SCARS

A Story Told in Pieces

Aditya Bhagchandani

Made with ❤ on the BookLeaf Publishing Platform
www.bookleafpub.in
www.bookleafpub.com

Dedication

Sometimes, life leaves behind scars so deep that no matter how much time passes, they never fully heal. Traumatic experiences, especially in childhood, shape the way we see the world, often making us push away the people who matter most.

This book is for those who have loved but never got closure, for those whose stories remain unfinished—whether because of fate, the past, or circumstances beyond their control. **Even when love is lost, its echoes stay with us forever.**

Preface

Love is often painted as something eternal, something that always finds its way back. But sometimes, love isn't about forever—it's about the moments that shaped us, the emotions we couldn't control, and the choices we never had the power to change.

This book is not just a collection of poems; it's a journey of two souls who met, loved, and lost. It explores the complexities of love and trauma, how the past lingers in the present, and how fate often plays a game of its own. Through every encounter, every unspoken word, and every decision made or left unfinished, this story reflects the reality that not all love stories find a perfect ending.

Some stories remain incomplete, yet their echoes are never truly silent…

Acknowledgements

Doing something for the first time is never easy, but the excitement of the journey always makes it worthwhile. The writer in me is finally getting the chance to be heard, and this moment wouldn't have been possible without the support of my family, my close friends, and Krishna Ji.

Special mention to my brother, Manish - Because I love him the most!

I hope this book reaches everyone who has inspired me—whether knowingly or unknowingly. A heartfelt thank you to those who have always listened to my words, whether in the form of poetry, stories, or fleeting thoughts. Your presence and encouragement have meant more than I can express.

And finally, here's to life—where my journey is still unfolding. Until then, let's continue unlocking every dream we've ever wished to achieve.

1. There She Stood

Down the street on a quiet day,
he walked alone, lost in his way.
Then like a dream, like fate's own art,
she stood there, stealing his heart.

A fleeting glance, a gasp, a pause—
his heart retraced the steps once lost.
Years had passed, yet there she stood,
time had touched but not withstood.

She looks the same, maybe a bit older,
the winds of time had brushed her shoulders.
Yet in her eyes, the light still shone,
a story lived, yet still unknown.

2. Shadow

There she stood, still and bright,
he could gaze at her till morning light.
But did she feel it too, just like him,
or was he lost in what once had been?

Did her hands recall the streets they walked,
the words they spoke, the dreams once talked?
Or was he just a shadow now,
a face in crowds she won't allow?

Did her heart race just like his,
or had it settled into peace?
Was this moment his alone,
a past she'd left, a love outgrown?

He longed to speak, yet fear remained,
uncertain what fate had reclaimed.
Was love now shaping something new,
or was second chapter closing too?

3. When Eyes Met

The first time they met, just like this,
a fleeting glance, a brush with bliss.
But then the roads were busy, loud,
yet still, she stood out from the crowd.

The noise felt distant, yet so near,
when their eyes met, the world turned clear.
No words were spoken, none were planned,
yet he knew—he'd found her hand.

That night, he walked with something new,
a stirring fire, a world in bloom.
Each flower whispered of her grace,
each raindrop traced her soft embrace.

The city's hum became her song,
each step he took, she walked along.
The golden dusk, the silver dawn,
all spoke of her, though she was gone

And so, before their words were shared,
before their hands had touched the air,
she lived within each breath he drew,
a love he felt before he knew.

4. Fate

They met beneath the city's glow,
where silent hearts began to know.
A glance, a spark, a world so new,
before they spoke, their souls just knew.

She loved the sound of autumn leaves,
he loved how she would roll her sleeves.
She'd hum a tune when days felt long,
he'd write her name into his songs.

He brought her roses, just because,
she'd steal his jacket when it was cold.
She'd trace his palm, a little game,
he'd blush whenever she said his name.

But love is light, and luck is fire,
he played his hand, yet fate stood higher.
Luck's own hands can twist and bend,
but who decides how stories end?

5. Light

He remembers the first hello,
her voice so soft, the winds let go.
The silence broke, their hearts took flight,
as faces glowed in golden light.

The winter once so cold and bare,
the summer heat he couldn't bear.
Autumn winds and springtime's hue,
now felt alive, now sang anew.

And so it went, the days the years,
the same old streets, the same frontiers.
Yet love had painted all so bright,
turning shadows into light.

6. Whisper

She spoke at last, her voice so low,
like fading echoes in the snow.
He listened close, each word so thin,
as if she feared to let him in.

"I came here when I was nine,
the city dark, the streets unkind.
But in my home, I felt no fear,
until my world fell out of gear.

Thirteen years, too young to see,
the love I dreamed was never free.
My father left, my mother cried,
I learned that love was built on lies."

She sighed, the winter's chill grew deep,
the winds had tales she couldn't keep.
"They whisper still, they bite, they call,
reminding me of things once small."

She never stayed, she never tried,
no hand to hold, no arms to guide.
Yet somehow now, she stood right here,
with words unspoken, lost in fear.

But something made her stay this time,
a fleeting thought she couldn't find.
His eyes—they held a warmth so rare,
like something good had once been there.

7. The Moment

He spoke:

"The city rushed, the world moved fast,
but you walked alone, untouched, unasked.
Your eyes held stories, lost in time,
and fate had placed your steps near mine."

She smiled:

"The world had men who looked, then passed,
but your gaze was one that chose to last.
Not to claim, nor steal, nor own,
but to see the girl behind the stone."

8. Impatient Heart

He sat in silence, yet words ran wild,
his heart impatient, his thoughts a child.

*"Tell me your story, every part,
the days before, the love, the scars."*

*"Why do you walk through life alone?
Who held your heart? Where has it gone?"*

He watched her lips, he read her eyes,
searching for truths she left behind.

*"What do you seek in love so rare?
A touch, a promise, a world to share?"*

He longed to be the man she dreamed,
to fit the love she once believed.

9. Where Shall We Start?

He thought his questions came too soon,
yet there she sat beneath the moon.
No hesitation, no retreat,
just words she couldn't wait to speak.

"I don't know why, but with you, I don't hold back,
My words just flow, no fear, no track.
Something in you turns my mind unkind,
Steals my sleep, leaves my heart blind."

She leaned in close, her voice so light,
a whisper dancing through the night.
"But tell me first, where shall we start?
My days before, the love, or the scars?"

10. Beginning

He smiled, his heart a restless tide,
liking her more with every stride.

*"Tell me your story, your days before,
the childhood streets, the dreams you wore."*

*"Tell me where you grew, the place you call home,
the fears you hide, the joys you've known.*

*How is life with your mother near?
In this rushing city, do you disappear?"*

*"What do you love? What keeps you awake?
What makes you smile? What makes you break?"*

His heart was fast, though love was far,
but in her voice, he'd found a star.

11. Puzzle

"To know me," she sighed, "is not so light,
I am a puzzle of dark and bright.
The smallest joys can make me sing,
but the tiniest cracks can break my wing."

"My childhood was a world so sweet,
a jam-filled home where love ran deep.
Like jam that binds two pieces tight,
with flavor rich, with warmth so right."

"But you know well how stories change,
how love can slip, how hearts estrange.
That part I'll tell when time is due,
for now, let me share the rest with you."

"I write my dreams in pages wide,
once for a job, now from inside.
A poet now, I spill my soul,
yet even ink can't make me whole."

"The fantasies I spin and weave,
the worlds I build, the lives I grieve—
you could read them all, and still not see,
not know what's truly meant for me."

"For wants are plenty, dreams run wild,
but needs hide quiet, soft and mild.
So tell me now, if you have the art—
can you find what fills my heart?"

12. Love and Scars

"My life would shine, my world be bright,
if my father had just held on tight.
If love had stayed, if vows had kept,
if my mother hadn't wept and wept."

"She stayed so silent, took the pain,
bore the bruises, hid the stains.
She let him stray, she let him lie—
was love so weak it could just die?"

"A lust over love, a fleeting fire,
was that enough to kill desire?
I've asked myself, I've cursed his name,
tell me—are all men the same?"

"I hated him, I hated love,
watched my mother break, yet rise above.
But the scars he left, they don't erase,
they hide in corners, still take space."

13. Comfort

*"I have never known what love should be,
not in stories, not in dreams.
But in these days of knowing you,
I feel something quiet, something true."*

*"Your little ways, the things you do—
running late, but laughing through.
Your love for mountains, soft and still,
a dream you hold, a distant thrill."*

*"Is it too soon to say it all?
Perhaps too fast, perhaps too small.
But in this city, once so wide,
I find my comfort by your side."*

*"Yet before the road can start to bend,
before we call this more than friends,
I need to know the man you are,
to take the time, to hear your heart."*

14. Before We Walk

"The pain you went through was maybe a season,
but your smiles should have a deeper reason."
"I'm glad you speak with a heart so clear,
so precise, so raw, with nothing to fear."

"And yes, you should know before we go too far,
before we step beyond who we are."
"The city's my home, where I belong,
soccer my second love, where I am strong."

"I stand by my mom, love my dad just the same,
a childhood simple, untouched by pain.
Poetry? I don't know a thing,
numbers and sports have been my string."

"Friends are few, but real and near,
life has been steady, nothing severe."
These are the things he tells at the start,
the rest, the truth—he saves that part.

15. Stay

They thought alike, they felt the same,
two restless hearts, now in one name.
Months had passed in fleeting days,
wrapped in laughter, lost in haze.

Her book was bound, her words took flight,
his numbers soared, his dreams shone bright.
The world had watched their stories rise,
two lives now woven, side by side.

Before fate could write its say,
before the winds could pull away,
they chose to walk, not drift, not sway—
they chose to stay, they chose to stay.

16. Temper

The years had passed, their love felt strong,
through highs and lows, they moved along.
Her mother smiled, knowing well,
this love was safe, this love could dwell.

But love can break where tempers rise,
where silence fades and truth collides.
That night he came, his heart undone,
his patience lost, his mind outrun.

Drunk on anger, heavy breath,
he spilled the words he once had kept.
A voice too sharp, a tone too high,
the love they knew began to die.

And then it happened—fast yet slow,
his hand rose high, yet struck no blow.
No touch, no harm, no lasting pain,
but still, the past had called her name.

The shadow fell, the years turned back,
to nights where love had turned to black.
A girl, once small, behind the door,
watching fists that bruised before.

She didn't wait, she didn't cry,
she didn't scream, she didn't try.
She ran—through hallways, through the night,
away from him, away from sight.

17. She was gone

Months had passed, yet time stood still,
his world was quiet, his nights grew chill.
He searched for her in streets they knew,
in cafés warm, where echoes flew.

He fought with fate, he fought with pain,
he wished to see her once again.
"I never hurt, I never struck,"
but knew too well—*that wasn't enough.*

He had known her fears, her past, her ache,
the ghosts she swore she'd never wake.
Yet in one moment, rage took hold,
and love, once bright, grew dim and cold.

Years went by, he begged, he tried,
hoping love had not yet died.
But fate was cruel, the truth was bare—
she was gone, she wasn't there.

No trace, no note, no final word,
just silence louder than he'd heard.
She left the city, erased her name,
as if their love had died in flame

18. One Last Chance

There she stood, the same old street,
where fate once wove their hearts to meet.
Then, the sun had kissed the air,
now the wind just lingered there.

Once so crowded, now just two,
love once bright, now lost from view.
The air that carried whispered dreams,
now searched for love in empty streams.

His hands shook, his words fell weak,
how do you mend what silence speaks?
Years had passed, yet here she stands—
was this an ending, or one last chance?

19. Pain

Sensing his struggle, she broke the space,
words flowing steady, no time to waste.

"It's not surprising that we meet," she said,
"but what's shocking is—you look the same instead."
"You still come here, this bar down the road,
I thought it was ours, but you made it your own."

"Before you think, before you speak,
I know your hands were never meant to seek.
But raised voices, moving fists—
they took me back to the pain I wished had missed."

"And so I ran, not from you,
but from the ghost that still felt true.
Yet life goes on, it always must,
we heal, we grow, we learn to trust."

"I know you're well, and so am I,
the city stayed, but I let it die.
And still, I'm happy, after all this space—
to have met you again, in this very place."

20. Breathe

Tears slipped down as he began to speak,
his voice unsteady, his heart felt weak.

"Can I just gaze, just for a while?
Can I breathe the air you breathe, just for this time?"
"Is this real? Are you truly here?
Or just another dream drawing near?"

With hesitation, he found his voice,
words trembling, lost in choice.
"That bar, that bar, the worst one now,
but I still go, I don't know how."

"I sit there each night, just to stay,
to hold on, to live another day.
Not for the place, not for the wine,
but for a hope—you'd come, just one more time."

"I'm a fool, I didn't ask,
how have you been, how have the years passed?"
"I know your books, I've read them all,
but tell me, where are you? Did life call?"

"Are you just traveling, just passing through?
Or did this city pull you back too?"

21. His Own?

How funny is this life we live,
it hides the things we'd die to give.
When we crave, they slip away,
but when hope fades, they find their way.

And in this play of life and chance,
there stands a soul in love's expanse.
One who loved, who lost, who stayed,
who bent, who broke, yet never swayed.

And if love retraced its steps once more,
stood again at the same old door,
how does it feel—was it fate?
Or just a story told too late?

But before he could ask, before he could say,
a voice so small took breath away.
"Mom!"—a child's call from down the street,
his heart stood still, skipped a beat.

His lips parted, yet words fell through,
was this fate, or something new?
Was she his past, or still his home?
Was the child a stranger—or his own?